Thoughts From A Window Pane

Corey G. Carolina

Copyright Page

Printed in the United States of America

First Printing, 2016
ISBN 978-0-9975092-1-2
Rise and Develop Publishing
PO Box 690181
Tulsa, OK 74169-0181
Visit- www.CoreyCarolina.com
Email-corey@coreycarolina.com
Thoughts From A Window Pane

Table of Contents

Intro

Thoughts From a Window Pane is a glimpse into the mind of Corey Carolina as he continued his journey of forgiving and healing while dealing with his father not being an active figure in his life as a child and into adulthood. Corey wrote a book titled, *The Absent Father* during the same time as he completed this book. His thought was that *Thoughts From a Window Pane* would be a complementary book to *The Absent Father* as this book shares his thoughts of his absent father and other situations that a child may encounter while growing up. This provocative look at the emotions of an adult who longed for a meaningful relationship with his father is inspiring and heartbreaking. Corey wants to promote writing about pains and struggles as a way to release oneself from the internal prison of hate, anger, insecurities, and doubt. This book is deeply personal and Corey's hope is that his pain and struggles will help motivate someone else to shoot for the moon because if you miss you will at least land amongst the clouds.

Thought One:
My Father Wasn't There, But
That's Cool

Thoughts From A Window Pane

My father wasn't there, but that's cool,
I do not even know where I would be without you,
My mom helped raise me,
The village helped raise me,
Now I am here to raise you,
My children are the reason I am here,
My children are the reason I fear,
Not being successful is not an option,
Success is the only option,

My father wasn't there, but that's cool,
I was raised to be here with you,
I was raised not to be a fool,
And to try to raise, you,

My father wasn't there, but that's cool,
The ladies and fellas that I run in to,
Have been better than you,
I still feel the love that everyone gives to me,
I still feel the hate that everyone gives to me,
Sometimes it's better than what you gave me,

My father wasn't there, but that's cool,
Everyday that I think about the tears that I dropped,
I think about why those tears ever dropped,
Was it worth the pain and struggle that I had?
Was it worth my mom having to serve as my dad,
Mother's Day, Father's Day, it's all the same to me,

Thoughts From A Window Pane

But you didn't even think enough of me to love me and be there for me,
My mom struggled her entire life,
Thank God she was able to become a wife,
But just think about what I am supposed to think about and when I am supposed to think about, you being in the house,
I was the man of the house but I could barely tie my own shoes,
I gave my mom money when she had the blues,
21 or 22 with hate in his heart; that was me,
Lord I am so glad that it's no longer me.

I am glad that I have changed and forgiven my dad for not having the brains to be there for me holding the rains,
To make sure that I use my brains to do the best things I could in my life,
Show me how to pick a wife, show me how to live life, show me how to love life and do things right,

Mother, why doesn't my father love me? That's what I asked her,
Why did I have to grow up feeling like a bastard?
My dad was there, my dad was there, in a state not that far from me,
But he did not show up to be a father to me,
Calling me every once in a while, two or three days after my birthday for his first born male child,
That's not acceptable,

Thoughts From A Window Pane

My father wasn't there, but that's cool,
He raised me up to go to school,
He raised me up to be cool,

But I am not talking about my Earth father, I am talking
about you,
The Lord above has shined on me,
He blessed me with two children to raise,
Hopefully I can help them have better days,

My father wasn't there, but that's cool,
My heart is so full but what is it full of,
Is it full of love?
Is it full of hate?
Is it full of things that I don't want to talk about?
Is it full of things that I don't want to think about going
that route?
When you ask me about my father 8-10 years ago, I just
felt like I didn't want to talk about it,
I didn't want to be about it, I didn't want to see about it, I
didn't want to even think about it,

It being, a relationship with my father,
My pain and struggle pushed me to write The Absent
Father,
My heart pushed me to write The Absent Father,
The Lord pushed me not to be an absent father.

Thought Two:
The Power Of The Pen

Thoughts From A Window Pane

I now see that love doesn't mean the same to you,
Your voice doesn't reach my ears on special occasions,
I am completely caught up in the pain that I feel from you,
Where is my father?
I am being bullied but you are not here,
I am having my heart broken but you are not here,
My mother is struggling but you are not here,
My brother is growing up with his brother as his father figure,
Father, where are you?
I call out your name with no returned answer,
My life would be so much better if you were here father but you are not,
I am forced to make my own decisions based on what I think is right,
Father, where are you?
It must not have been meant for us to know each other
But why is that,
I need my father and I know he needs me,
He needs my love,
I do not want to give up hope that you will be there for me or that I will be there for you,
I was given a heart so I can love you father,
I was given a mind so I could forgive you father,
Your absence touches every part of me,
Father, where are you?

Thought Three:
Who Did I Write The Absent Father For?

I decided to write the book titled, *The Absent Father* as a way to deal with all the hate and pain I experienced from my father not being there very often when I was a child and into adulthood. So, whom did I write The Absent Father for?

I wrote this book for all the boys and girls who have sat in their beds crying because their father was not there.

I wrote this book for that young boy who was called gay and bullied but he couldn't go home to cry to his father because he was absent.

I wrote this book for the 15-year-old girl who thought she fell in love with her soul mate but found out he was her nightmare.

I wrote this book for all the single mothers who are working hard everyday to give their children a better life.

I wrote this book for the young children whose father passed away and they are forever affected by the void of their father.

I wrote this book for the 15-year old boy who is angry at the fact his father is absent and feels that he is not good enough to receive his father's love.

It took me eight years to write this book but 35 years to live what I wrote. I share the story of thousands of children and adults. I wanted to share my story with you all with the hope that we can all learn to forgive and not blame ourselves for another person's action. I felt like I was in prison with the anger that I had. I felt that I could not be successful unless I forgave my father. I have now been blessed with a wonderful wife and two amazing children.

So what is important in my life? It is important that almost every night I get to bathe my children and put them to sleep. I get to hug and kiss my mother. I get to hold my children close and breathe their breath. I get to see the love in my wife's eyes.

Why did I write The Absent Father?

I wrote it for the world.

Thoughts From A Window Pane

Thought Four:
Elle's First Love Letter

Hello baby this is dad. I love you more than anything on Earth. Just the thought of seeing you makes me smile. I know a lot of people will love you but I want to be the first to write how much I love you. You are the best thing to ever happen to me. You have changed life for the better forever. I have not held you yet but I love you. Seeing you on the ultrasound has brought joy to my life. I will work the rest of my life to be a great example for you. I will love you, cherish you, provide for you, and one again love you.

There were a lot of tears to get to this point but it was all worth it. You are our miracle from God. You will be put on this Earth to do great things. You will change lives just with your kindness. Please remember that daddy loves you and no matter what, I will be there for you. You are so special to me and I know you will be as beautiful as your mother. One day when I am no longer here, I will be at peace that you will be here and I will always be with you honey.

Thought Five:
A Letter To Ellington

Greeting son, this is your father. I want to first thank you for choosing your mother and me. We both are so excited that you will be with us soon. I am writing this letter so you will know that daddy loves you. When I found out that your mother was expecting another baby, I was so happy. Once I found out that we were having a boy, I was even more excited. I was also scared. I was scared that I would not be the father that I need to be to raise you to become a man. I wanted to ensure that I raise you and your sister to the best of my ability. The thoughts in my head were centered on how would I provide a great future for you all.

I want you to know that I work everyday to make you proud. I want to live up to your expectations. I want you to know that I will always be here for you and our family. I promise to provide love, shelter, discipline, mentoring, etc.... You are my son and I cannot express how it feels to say that. I cannot wait to see your eyes because I know within your eyes are the souls of our ancestors. There are so many people who are waiting to meet you. They know that you are as special as your sister Elle. I love you and I am waiting for you to bless our family with your arrival.

Thought Six:
My Present Father Is Still Absent

Thoughts From A Window Pane

I see you everyday, but you are absent,
I walk past you everyday, but you are absent,
I say I love you and you say you love me, but you are absent,
We use to spend more time together, but you do not make time for me. You are absent.
Your hugs use to be tighter, but now they are absent,
Your kisses use to be warm, but now they are cold and forced because you are absent.
How can you be in the same room as me, but still be absent?
Do I not deserve your attention or will you continue to be absent?
My father is present but he is still absent.

Thought Seven:
My Single Mother Is Amazing

Thoughts From A Window Pane

From the womb, you birthed me after 36 hours of labor,
You frequently went to Wal-Mart with no money and went to the lotion isle and took a few squirts of lotion to put on my dry skin,
You risked your life for me to be able to be here today,
You are my shining star,
You are the first women I ever loved,
I learned how to be an entrepreneur from you,
I learned the importance of education from you,
You did not want me to grow up with dislike for my father,
You told me that no matter what, I needed to pray for my father,
I remember those days when the lights were off and we had to eat out of canned food,
I pray that one day, I can provide you with a personal chef to cook your food,
You did not have to put something hot to my backside very often,
But you gave me that look that only a mother can give,
As I write this poem I think about all you gave up to raise me,
You gave up your youth to raise me,
I am sure that you had big dreams that you did not get to realize,
I can never repay you for your great compromise,
I love you and I appreciate you.

Thought Eight:
Random Thoughts

Thoughts From A Window Pane

I was born to be brilliant but I have a learning disability,
My mind thinks in a different way from other people,
I see the world as an opportunity,
I am an eternal optimist,
I have a hard time remembering what I read and comprehending words,
I feel the Lord made me this way in order to drive me to be better,
I have a big heart but I am a jerk at times,
I see light in the dark and I see half a cup of opportunity in a half-filled cup,
My dreams are stories that should become movies,
Life for me has finally become clear and my purpose is shown,
Find your purpose and your voice shall follow.

Thought Nine:
The Absent Puzzle Piece

Thoughts From A Window Pane

Our family pictures are missing a key puzzle piece,
Where is my father? Why is he not in the picture with us?
He is the absent puzzle piece,
Our family is not a complete puzzle without our father,
Our family wall is not complete without my absent puzzle piece,
My mother, brother, and sister are here but there is still one piece missing,
How can I feel complete if a piece of me is missing?
Father, please come back into our lives and no longer be our absent puzzle piece.

Thought Ten:
My First Broken Heart

Thoughts From A Window Pane

My first broken heart was supposed to be that pretty girl with the long wavy hair, hazel eyes, beautiful smile, soft skin, sweet voice, big heart, and funny laugh. I was suppose to see the girl I liked walking down the hall at school and try to muster up the courage to ask for her phone number only to have her say no thank you and walk off. I was supposed to buy the girl I liked a valentine heart and chocolate only to have her say, "Thank you friend". My heart was supposed to be crushed when I walked in to class and saw my best friend hugging the girl I felt I loved.

These were the scenarios that were supposed to happen for me to have my first broken heart but instead my absent father broke my heart first. He was the first person to promise me that he would come to a football game and did not come. He was the first person to forget to call me on my birthday. He was the person who said he would be there for me but he wasn't.

Thought Eleven:
Mother, Why Doesn't My Father Love Me?

Thoughts From A Window Pane

Mother, why doesn't my father love me,
Why is he taking care of the new baby that he just fathered?
Am I not good enough to spend time with?
I am the first-born boy, why doesn't he love me?
I think I hate my father but I want him to love me,
I prayed that the Lord would make my father love me but he does not,
Mother, no boyfriend you bring around will ever love me like I want my father to love me,
I am so sad that my father doesn't love me,
You tell me that my father loves me but he never shows me,
Mother, why doesn't my father love me?

Thought Twelve:
Father From A Distance

My son will know me is what he said.
How is that possible when you don't even read books to him before bed?
You provide no support for your son but you act like you are the father of the year.
A real father sees his son more than one time each year,
You may live in a different household than your child
But that does not give you the excuse not to have a relationship with your child,
You blame your son's mother for you not being around,
Trust me, you are going to miss your child when you are placed underground,
A present father is essential to a child's life.
A father is essential to show a boy how to be a man and a girl how to be a woman.

Thought Thirteen:
$26

Life insurance is the key to financial wealth,
How many go fund me request do you get to help raise money for a funeral?
How many times have you helped cover expenses for a relative's funeral?
Why should someone else have to pay for another person's funeral?
It is that person's responsibility to cover the expenses of their funeral,
This is not the reality for most people,
There are millions of people who are not covered by life insurance and that is not fair to their families.
The way that even a middle-income person can help transfer wealth is for them to have life insurance.
Take this scenario, a person has a $10,000 policy and that person passes.
It costs from $10,000-$15,000 to bury that person so the family is going to have to come up with the other money to bury their loved one. The family must take away from their own savings to help bury a loved one who did not ensure that their funeral expenses were covered.
If only the family member could have gotten a life insurance policy for $26 per month, that insurance policy could have covered the funeral expenses.
A difference between some in the middle class and others in upper class is the wealth that is transferred. Poor or middle class individuals either do not have life insurance to cover their funeral expenses or they have a policy that just covers enough. Upper class individuals pay for their funeral expenses in advance and have a $250,000-

$500,000 policy to set their family up for financial success.

The middle class and even the poor should try to get a policy that will not only cover their funeral expenses but also leave money to the remaining family to assist with changing lives. The insurance policy could now allow a surviving spouse or child the opportunity to move out of substandard housing and allow the children in the household to go to a quality school. That now changes the history the children and can potentially set their future on course for success. This can all be achieved for $26 per month.

Thoughts From A Window Pane

Thought Fourteen: I Don't Need Him

Thoughts From A Window Pane

I am grown and I do not need him,
He was not there for me, so I do not need him,
I help my mother pay the bills, so I do not need him,
I am the man of the house, so I do not need him,
He chose to be the father to other kids and forget about
me, so I do not need him,
He decided to love them but beat me, so I do not need
him,
I look like him, but I do not need him,
I am so angry with my father, but I do not need him,
I wish I could cry on his shoulder, but I do not need him,
I wish I could tell him I love him, but I do not need him,
My father is not here, but now I see I do need him.

Thought Fifteen:
How Does A Man Become An Absent Father?

So how does a man become an absent father?

My father was raised by both his mother and father but he was absent,

An absent father starts with that moment of passion with the person you feel you will be with the rest of your life only to find out that he is your worst choice ever. You find out that he is an alcoholic, you find out that he is an abuser, you find out you are pregnant, and finally you find out that he is going to be an absent father. My father went to college and graduated. He was a star athlete with all the talent in the world, but he was an absent father.

So how does a man become an absent father?

It happens with one argument where the father has had enough of dealing with the mother. He decides that his child is not worth all of the headaches that he feels the mother brings. He has made the decision to give up. His child will now be made to grow up without the love and comfort of his/her father. This is all because the mother and father could not act like adults and work things out to at least both be present in their child's life. Adults make childish decisions related to working out conflict even when it affects children. Can an absent father become present if he and the mother are able to speak to each other and get past some of the issues that caused the father to back away? It is not more important to win the argument. It is more important to win the battle of raising a child to graduate college and become a productive adult. That is success.

Thought Sixteen:
Jordan 401K

What will you leave your child when you die?
Will you leave 58 pairs of Jordan shoes and bills that they must pay? Or will you leave your child a 401K, rental properties, business royalties, life insurance, and a positive memory of you,
Our children do not have to be in the newest Jordan's to feel loved,
They need a secure future financially,
What have you done to ensure that your child does not have to struggle as much as you or your parent did?
Remember the term, "Pay yourself first".
That means that when you get a paycheck, take out a portion to save for emergencies.
The Jordan 401K will not help your children succeed.
The financial 401K will help your children have a good head start.
The next time you think about buying those Jordan's for your child or yourself, ask yourself if you have a plan for putting back money for your child to be successful.

Thought Seventeen: I Forgive You Father

Thoughts From A Window Pane

You forgot about me, but I forgive you father,
You mentally and physically abused me, but I forgive you father,
You left my mother to raise my siblings by herself, but I forgive you father,
You never call me, but I forgive you father,
You were absent, but I forgive you father,
I hated you for 27 years, but I now forgive you father,
My mother was hurt by you, but she forgives you father,
I was beat up by a bully and you were nowhere to be found, but I forgive you father,
I lost my first child to a miscarriage and you were nowhere to be found, but I forgive you father,
My life has been lost without you, but I forgive you father,
I am a sinner and I pray the Lord forgives me so it is only right that I forgive you father.

Thought Eighteen: My Fears

When I found out that my wife was pregnant, I instantly had two emotions. I was so happy and I had a huge sense of fear. My father did not raise me, my mother and my village did. I asked myself, "How am I going to be a good parent to this baby girl". I was scared that I would fail. This is an emotion that so many fathers have. We question ourselves by asking, "Will we be good enough". I had to figure out how I was going to support my wife emotionally and be there to help with my daughter. I remember crying uncontrollably the first night we brought our baby home. All of my emotions about miscarriages just came out at one time. I think it surprised my wife because she had only seen me cry at funerals. She just held me as all of my fears, heartaches, disappointment, and anger poured out of my body. I firmly believe that sometimes you just need a good cry.

I remember the first time that I walked into the operating room as the doctors and staff prepared my wife for delivery of our first child. I wanted to make sure I kept a smile on my face so my wife would be encouraged but inside, I was so scared that I felt like I was going to be sick. First off, the medical professionals had her on this table that seemed so small. There was the blue sheet hanging which was covering my wife's lower body. The scene was just like what I had seen on the television show about pregnancy and delivery. It felt so weird to actually be in the room. I knew that I wanted nothing more than to be by my wife's side as she helped bring life into this world but it was scary. I feared that something would happen to my wife or my baby. I prayed different times during the delivery. The Lord brought my wife and baby through safely. When the nurse handed me my daughter, I did not know how I should hold her. She was real. I had practiced holding dolls during parenting classes but those dolls were not real. She looked up at me and my heart melted. I said to myself, "my baby is here". I instantly fell in love with her. At that time, I could only think about taking care of her for the rest of my life and how that was my greatest honor.

The Lord blessed me even though I was a sinner. He blessed me with the opportunity to participate in the joy of parenthood. I had been angry with the Lord due to our past miscarriages but I apologized to him for being angry and I communicated with him that I will trust in his plan for my wife and I. Her eyes opened to see her father. She had screamed so loudly when she was pull out of my wife's stomach but when I held her, she stopped. She heard my voice during pregnancy and realized that I was the one she had heard. Even though she was born three years ago, I still get tearful when I think about or write about her.

A couple years later, we were blessed again with my first-born boy. The day that we went in for the ultrasound to reveal the gender of our baby, I was so nervous. I of course told people that I would be happy no matter the gender but deep inside, I was pulling for a boy. When the ultrasound tech told us it was a boy, I was overjoyed. The

Lord had blessed me again but I was so fearful. I asked myself, "How are you going to raise your boy to become a man"?

Thought Nineteen:
I Cry Because I Am Happy

Thoughts From A Window Pane

When I think about my children being born, I cry
When I listen to a song that hits my heart, I cry
Every time I think about how good God has been to me, I cry,
When I see young people following their dreams, I cry
When I think about my grandmother's homemade hamburgers, I cry
I cry because I am happy,
I cry because I think about all the things that I have been blessed with,
I cry because even though I am a sinner, I have more than I deserve,
I cry because my children run up to me every time they see me,
I cry when I sit and think about what God has in store for me,
I cry when I think about the great future my children will have,
I cry when I think about all of the people who Qianna, Karla, and myself have helped,
I cry when I think about all the support great people have given us over the years,
I cry because I am happy.

Thought Twenty:
I Cry Because I Am Sad

When I think about the struggles that my mother had growing up, I cry

When I think about the little boy who will grow up to become a murderer, I cry

When I think about all the hate in our world, I cry

When I think about the little girl, who will lose her life in a bomb attack, I cry

When I think about the 15 million children who live in single mother households, I cry

When I think about the people who have to deal with a miscarriage, I cry

I cry when I am sad,

I cry when I think about the young man, who has great grades but will never graduate high school,

I cry when I think about that mother, who has to bury her child,

I cry when I think about the absent father who will never have the joy that I feel with my children.

Thought Twenty-One:
The Deaf Eye

Springtime dew shines with the rising sun over the mountains and under the clouds. The chilly wind blows at a cool 63 degrees while the butterflies flap their wings. A child wakes to the shutters clapping back and forth. The breeze feels like God is gently whispering. The birds are singing as if they are bringing the gospel. As the child cuddles up with her favorite teddy bear, she feels comforted.

You see, this child is a victim of child abuse. The world may seem beautiful to the outside person but to her, the world will never be the same. Her view is different. She does not see the dew as it shines under the sunlight. She only sees dark clouds. The shutters clapping scare her because they bring back bad memories. The birds are crows and ravens that are screaming at her. She clings to her bear because that is the only friend she has. Her mother, brother, and her uncle took a deaf eye to her abuse. They did not believe what they heard and they did not believe what they saw. Her innocent childhood was taken and the people who were suppose to be there to hear her and watch her decided to have The Deaf Eye.

Thought Twenty-Two: Bully

Thoughts From A Window Pane

You thought because you picked on me, that I would fail,
You were not only my bully, but you were also my motivator,
You motivated me to get strong, find my voice, and stand up for what I believed,
You picked on me because I was different,
You chose to hit me because you were jealous of me,
You did not know that I would grow up to be a successful person,
What have you achieved in life? Nothing!
I hope you felt important when you bullied me,
I refused to let you dictate the life I would have,
You are not a factor to me any longer,
My bully is real and he was a mean little boy,
As I think about it, I wonder how things were at his home,
Did he have a loving mother who sacrificed everything for him?
Did he have an absent father?
Did he get hugged enough?
I feel sorry for him that he had to make himself feel better by picking on someone smaller than him,
Children are being bullied everyday either in person or online,
If you have a bully for a husband or boyfriend, remember what your children will be learning,
Bullies have killed and been killed,
Save our youth by keeping a close eye on your child to monitor if he or she is a bully or being bullied.
You may save a life.

Thought Twenty-Three: I Am Poor And No One Loves Me

Thoughts From A Window Pane

Mom, we are poor and no one loves us,
Mom, I am poor and no one loves me,
Why do we have to eat from the Popeye spinach can?
Why do we have to eat leftovers?
I want to be like the other kids but I can't because I am poor,
I can't succeed like them because I am poor,
I will not live as many years as them because I am poor,
Mom, why did God make us poor and them rich?
Mom, why do I have to walk to school and their parents drive them to school,
Mom, why do I have to watch my brother overnight while you go to work,
I am scared to be home at night,
I hear people say that poor people are not helping the economy,
Mom, why are we not helping the economy?

Son, you are not poor, you are special,
Since you have had to struggle, you will know how it feels to be poor and you will never want to be poor when you grow up,
Son, you are the key to getting us out of this neighbor,
Son, you have to make good grades so you can help your mom get out of this neighborhood,
Son, if it wasn't for the poor people working hard at the jobs they have, the rich people would not be as rich,
Son, you are just as rich as the next boy. You are rich in health. You are able to dress yourself daily, you are able to walk without assistance, and have God.

Thoughts From A Window Pane

Never let anyone make you feel less than your worth. There are rich people who were poor before they were rich.

They worked hard, made contacts with other people, and did not allow anyone to tell them that their dream wasn't attainable.

Son, you dream of being rich one day and that can happen if you do these things,

You must pray daily, believe in yourself, educate yourself, come up with a good idea, and treat others fairly.

Son, I am here to push you, support you, and advise you.

You are poor in the sense of money but baby you are the riches little boy I know with potential, faith, and love for your mom. I love you son.

Thoughts From A Window Pane

Thought Twenty-Four:
Pregnant And Scared

My stomach is tight and I am so scared,
I went to the doctor and he said there might be a baby growing,
How will I take care of this baby?
I have never been a parent,
I ask myself, "How did this happen?" but I know how it happened,
I feel myself about to throw up,
My skin color is pale like a ghost has scared me,
I am not ready for this,
What will my mother say?
What will she think about me?
She always told me that a baby would be difficult to raise,
I do not want to do this?
I contemplate my options and none seems optimal,
Pregnant and Scared is an understatement,
Pregnant and Terrified is more appropriate,
I lay in the bed and I cannot sleep thinking about the child that I may be bringing into the world,
My mom's baby may be having a baby and I do not know how to feel about that,

I just decided that I wanted to be back with my significant other and this happens,
How do I explain that I may become a parent?
I just had a great make up date with my ex but there is no way we will be able get back together now,
My life can be changed for the rest of my days on Earth,
Should I feel bad that I hope the doctor tells me that a baby is not growing?

Thoughts From A Window Pane

I pray my future will not be altered tomorrow after the
doctor's visit,
Life is.........

Thoughts From A Window Pane

Thought Twenty-Five:
The Third-Grade Felon

Prisons are built in areas where the third-grade test scores and grades are at a failing level,

Private prisons make money on our children living the life of a third-grade felon,

Statistics show that if our child is failing third grade, it is likely that he/she will become an inmate in prison.

Statistics show that if our child doesn't have a father in the home, that child is at a greater risk of becoming an inmate in prison.

It's not cute that our children look fly in new Jordan's but makes the grades that are guiding them to a track of incarceration.

Not all felons are dumb.

Some are brilliant but they just made a bad decision.

The third-grade felon is a reality in so many communities across America.

We must focus on early education of our children. We must do everything we can do to prevent them from becoming a third-grade felon. We must love them, discipline them, and guide them to success. Our third graders can become graduates, entrepreneurs, teachers, police officers, or they can become third grade felons.

Thought Twenty-Six:
I Died An Absent Father

I fathered four children, whom I never built a relationship with,

I never was there to wish them a happy birthday,

I did not get to walk my daughters down the isle when they got married,

I did not see my babies walk across the stage at graduation,

My life was filled with nothingness,

I died an absent father,

My children never got to hear all of the great stories from my childhood,

My children never got to hear how proud of them I was,

My children just wanted their father and I was never there,

I let them down but they still came to my funeral to wish me to a peaceful afterlife,

I left my babies to be raised by their mothers and I never instilled my values into their lives,

I died an absent father. I died alone without the love of my children filling my heart,

I was so lost and selfish when they were born. I did not even go to the hospital when they were born. I was too worried about proving that I was not their father instead of loving them and holding them tightly.

I died an absent father. I spent 83 years on the Earth trying to find a meaning for my life and it was right in front of me. My purpose was to raise my children to be productive adults and I failed at that. They were successful despite my absence. I am happy and sad about that.

My babies grew up without their father and now I am dead. I give all credit to their mothers. Without them, my children may have gone down the wrong road. My life has ended but theirs lives on so I died happy.

Thoughts From A Window Pane

Thought Twenty-Seven: The Absent Grandfather

Thoughts From A Window Pane

You were an absent father and I forgave you for that,
You were not there for me when I needed you and I
forgave you for that,
You broke my mother's heart and I forgave you for that,
But now, you do not try to have a relationship with my
children, I can't forgive you for that,
It is not okay to be an Absent Grandfather,
No excuse is expectable,
When you see my children, they should remind you of
how blessed you are,
Instead you look at them like they are children of a
stranger,
When does being absent change for you?
When will you step up and take your proper role of the
head of the family?
When will you finally try to raise children?
My children mean the world to me and I want them to
mean the world to you,
I guess that is a fantasy,
My children bring joy to the lives they touch but they have
brought you no joy,
You were not there when they were born, you did not
come to one baby shower, and you have yet to tell them
you love them,
My Absent Father is an Absent Grandfather,
I hoped that as years passed, you would have grown to see
what is most important,
Family is all you have and you act like your grandchildren
do not exists,

Thoughts From A Window Pane

My mother has always told me to continue to pray for you, which I will continue to do,
My children deserve to know who their grandfather is but you are robbing them of that option,
My Absent Father is an Absent Grandfather.

Thoughts From A Window Pane

Thought Twenty-Eight:
The Absent Mother

Thoughts From A Window Pane

I thought you were supposed to always be there but you weren't,

That comment is usually made about fathers but it applies to you mother,

You aren't there for me when I need you,

I hurt and you are only worried about your boyfriend and your friends,

You leave me alone for hours while you enjoy your time with your friends,

You never tell me I am pretty,

I think that I am a nuisance to you,

All I wanted was to have a better mother- daughter relationship and you refuse to give me that,

Your milk kept me alive, your love kept me warm, but your neglect keeps tears running down my face.

Mother, where were you when that girl and her friends hit and kicked me until I passed out,

Mother, where were you when the group of young boys grabbed my butt and breast and laughed,

Mother, where were you when my first love beat me and my children while you acted like you could not see my bruises,

Mother you were absent to me even though we lived in the same house,

Life with you would have been better if you never raised me and I just thought that you were my next-door neighbor.

Thoughts From A Window Pane

Thoughts From A Window Pane